A Quick Guide to…

Gender Mainstreaming
in the Public Service

Commonwealth Secretariat

Gender Management System Series

Gender Management System Handbook

Using Gender-Sensitive Indicators: A Reference Manual for Governments and Other Stakeholders

Gender Mainstreaming in Development Planning: A Reference Manual for Governments and Other Stakeholders

Gender Mainstreaming in Finance: A Reference Manual for Governments and Other Stakeholders

Gender Mainstreaming in the Public Service: A Reference Manual for Governments and Other Stakeholders

Gender Mainstreaming in Education: A Reference Manual for Governments and Other Stakeholders

Gender Mainstreaming in Trade and Industry: A Reference Manual for Governments and Other Stakeholders

Gender Mainstreaming in Agriculture and Rural Development: A Reference Manual for Governments and Other Stakeholders

Gender Mainstreaming in Information and Communications: A Reference Manual for Governments and Other Stakeholders

Gender and Equal Employment Opportunities: A Reference Manual for Governments and Other Stakeholders

A Quick Guide to the Gender Management System

A Quick Guide to Using Gender-Sensitive Indicators

A Quick Guide to Gender Mainstreaming in Development Planning

A Quick Guide to Gender Mainstreaming in Finance

A Quick Guide to Gender Mainstreaming in the Public Service

A Quick Guide to Gender Mainstreaming in Education

A Quick Guide to Gender Mainstreaming in Trade and Industry

A Quick Guide to Gender Mainstreaming in Agriculture and Rural Development

A Quick Guide to Gender Mainstreaming in Information and Communications

A Quick Guide to Gender and Equal Employment Opportunities

Commonwealth Secretariat
Marlborough House
Pall Mall, London SW1Y 5HX,
United Kingdom

© Commonwealth Secretariat,
June 1999

Designed and published by the Commonwealth Secretariat.
Printed in the United Kingdom by Abacus Direct.
Wherever possible, the Commonwealth Secretariat uses paper sourced from sustainable forests or from sources that minimise a destructive impact on the environment.

Copies of this publication can be ordered direct from:

Vale Packaging Ltd,
420 Vale Road, Tonbridge, Kent
TN9 1TD, United Kingdom
Tel: + 44 (0)1732 359387
Fax: +44 (0) 1732 770620
e-mail: vale@vale-ltd.co.uk

Price: £5.99
0-85092-597-5

Web sites:
http://www.thecommonwealth.org/gender
http://www.thecommonwealth.org
http://www.youngcommonwealth.org

Contents

List of Tables

Preface

In 1996, Commonwealth Ministers Responsible for Women's Affairs mandated the Commonwealth Secretariat to develop the concept of the Gender Management System (GMS), a comprehensive network of structures, mechanisms and processes for bringing a gender perspective to bear in the mainstream of all government policies, programmes and projects. The establishment and strengthening of gender management systems and of national women's machineries was the first of 15 government action points identified in the 1995 Commonwealth Plan of Action on Gender and Development.

This guide is intended to assist readers in using a GMS to mainstream gender in the public service ministry of national governments. It is an abridged version of the GMS publication *Gender Mainstreaming in the Public Service: A Reference Manual for Governments and Other Stakeholders* presenting the main points of that document in an accessible way. It is hoped that both documents will be used by public service commissioners, personnel managers, planners, field staff and others.

These publications are part of the Gender Management System Series, which provides tools and sector-specific guidelines for gender mainstreaming. This guide is intended to be used in combination with other documents in the GMS Series, particularly the *Gender Management System Handbook,* which presents the conceptual and methodological framework of the GMS.

The development of the GMS Reference Manuals and Quick Guides has been a collaborative effort between the Commonwealth Secretariat's Gender and Youth Affairs Division and many individuals and groups. Their contributions to the thinking behind the GMS are gratefully acknowledged. In particular, I would like to thank the following: all those member governments who supported the development of the GMS and encouraged us to move the project forward; participants at the first GMS meeting in Britain in February 1997 and at the GMS Workshop in Malta in April 1998, who provided invaluable conceptual input and feedback; and the Steering Committee on the Plan of Action (SCOPA). I am also most grateful to: the various consultants who wrote and edited the text of the guide, including Commissioner Hope Sadza of the Zimbabwe Public Service Commission and Daniel Woolford, Consultant Editor of the GMS Series; Alex Matheson, Special Advisor in the Management and Training Services Division, Commonwealth Secretariat, who provided valuable comments and input; and the staff of the Gender Affairs Department, Gender and Youth Affairs Division, Commonwealth Secretariat, particularly Ms Eleni Stamiris, former Director of the Division, who took the lead in formulating the GMS concept and mobilising the various stakeholders in its development, Dr Judith May-Parker who provided substantive editorial input, and Dr Rawwida Baksh-Soodeen, Project Co-ordinator of the GMS Series, who guided the project through to publication.

We hope that this resource series will be of genuine use to you in your efforts to mainstream gender.

Nancy Spence
Director
Gender and Youth Affairs Division
Commonwealth Secretariat

1 Introduction

Gender and the Public Service

Despite major efforts and some progress over the last couple of decades, women continue to be disadvantaged in comparison with men in many aspects of life, in most countries. The UNDP's Human Development Report records progress in human development according to indicators of health, education and income. Since 1995 the Human Development Index has included two gender-related indexes: the Gender-Related Development Index and the Gender Empowerment Measure (GEM). The GEM is of particular significance to the public service because it focuses on women's and men's political participation (seats held in parliament), the percentages of administrators and managers, and professional and technical workers who are women, and the share of earned income going to women and men. Thus, although the figures used in the GEM relate not just to the public sector but to all sectors, they provide a snapshot of the gender breakdown of decision-making in various countries, which informs an understanding of how women fare relative to men within the public service itself.

Table 1 shows the GEM for selected Commonwealth countries. It reveals that while in some countries women are well represented among professional and technical staff, there are fewer women than men working as parliamentarians, administrators and managers in all Commonwealth countries for which figures are available. And in terms of earned income share, the picture in most areas is of significant bias in favour of men.

Gender Mainstreaming

The 1995 Commonwealth Plan of Action on Gender and Development presents a vision of:

Table 1   **Gender Empowerment Measure (GEM), Selected Commonwealth Countries**

Country	GEM Rank	Seats Held in Parliament (% to Women)	Adminins-trators and Managers (% Women)	Professional and Technical Workers (% Women)	Earned Income Share (% toWomen)
Australia	11	20.5	43.3	25.0	39.8
The Bahamas	19	10.8	26.3	56.9	39.5
Bangladesh	76	9.1	5.1	23.1	23.1
Barbados	14	18.4	37.0	52.1	39.5
Belize	32	10.8	36.6	38.8	18.0*
Botswana	39	8.5	36.1	61.4	38.9
Cameroon	65	12.2	10.1	24.4	30.9
Canada	6	19.3	42.2	56.1	37.8
Cyprus	60	5.4	10.2	40.8	27.1
Fiji Islands	68	5.8	9.6	44.7	21.4
Guyana	33	20.0	12.8	47.5	26.4
India	86	7.3	2.3	20.5	25.7
Lesotho	41	11.2	33.4	56.6	30.3
Maldives	67	6.3	14.0	34.6	35.4
Malta	-	-	-	-	20.9
Malawi	80	5.6	4.8	34.7	42.0
Malaysia	48	10.3	11.9	44.5	30.2
Mauritius	49	7.6	14.3	41.4	25.4
Mozambique	43	25.2	11.3	20.4	41.3
New Zealand	5	29.2	32.3	47.8	38.8
Pakistan	92	3.4	3.4	20.1	20.8
Papua New Guinea	85	-	11.6	29.5	34.8
Sierra Leone	77	6.3	8.0	32.0	29.7
Singapore	47	2.5	34.3	16.1	30.7
Solomon Islands	91	2.1	2.6	27.4	40.0*
South Africa	22	23.7	17.4	46.7	30.8
Sri Lanka	70	5.3	16.9	24.5	34.5
Swaziland	61	8.4	14.5	54.3	34.9
Trinidad & Tobago	17	19.4	23.3	53.3	29.7
United Kingdom	20	7.8	33.0	43.7	35.0
Zambia	71	9.7	6.1	31.9	38.8
Zimbabwe	45	14.7	15.4	40.0	37.4

"a world in which women and men have equal rights and opportunities at all stages of their lives to express their creativity in all fields of human endeavour, and in which women are respected and valued as equal and able partners in establishing values of social justice, equity, democracy and respect for human rights. Within such a framework of values, women and men will work in collaboration and partnership to ensure people-centred sustainable development for all nations."

Commonwealth Secretariat, 1995

Gender mainstreaming is the central strategy of the Plan of Action for advancing gender equality and equity. It refers to the consistent use of a gender perspective at all stages of the development and implementation of policies, plans, programmes and projects. In terms of the public service, this would include the activities of the public service commission, the central personnel office of government, as well as personnel departments in core and sectoral ministries.

Scope and Objectives of this Guide

The purpose of this publication is to provide guidelines for mainstreaming gender in the public service of national governments.

The guide presents the main elements of the Gender Management System, which has been developed by the Commonwealth as an effective means of mainstreaming gender in national governments and in the broader civil society. It provides an overview of global and Commonwealth mandates for promoting gender equality and equity, and examines the development of theoretical approaches to the issue.

The guide examines the structures and functions of public service personnel management in the context of public service reform, and examines gender-related policy issues in personnel management. And it provides guidelines on gender analysis and proposes a number of policy interventions which governments may consider adopting, depending on particular national circumstances, to advance gender equality and equity in the public service. It is intended primarily for use by Commonwealth governments that are implementing gender mainstreaming in all their policies, plans and programmes. It may also be of use to other governments, related agencies and non-governmental organisations.

* to nearest whole number
- figures not available
Source: United Nations Development Programme, 1997

2 The Context

Mandates for Gender Equality and Equity

Advancing gender equality and equity has been mandated internationally by the Commonwealth, by the UN and related agencies, and by some regional groupings.

The Commonwealth

The Commonwealth is committed to gender equality and equity. The central strategy of the 1995 Commonwealth Plan of Action on Gender and Development is the mainstreaming of gender considerations into all government policies, programmes and projects. The Plan of Action advocates the adoption by member governments of a national gender action plan, and emphasises the importance of a strong national women's machinery, with authority emanating from the highest level of government and adequate resources, to lead the mainstreaming process.

Among 15 government action points under the Plan of Action, seven are of particular relevance to public service commissions, central personnel offices, and similar government agencies:

1   establish and strengthen gender management systems and national women's machineries;
2   integrate gender issues in all national policies, plans and programmes;
3   build capacity in gender planning;
4   become a model of good practice as a gender-aware employer;
5   promote equal opportunities and positive and/or affirmative action throughout the country and consult women and men equally on priorities;
6   take action for anti-discrimination;
7   take action for women's participation in decision-making.

As key players in the staffing of governments and the management of personnel in the public service – with responsibilities that can include appointments, promotions, training and discipline – public service commissions and central personnel offices are strategically placed to carry out these action points and make a significant contribution to advancing gender equality, both directly (within government) and indirectly (in the wider society).

Global commitments

The Platform for Action adopted by the 1995 Fourth World Conference on Women in Beijing called upon governments, the international community and civil society to take action on 12 critical areas of concern, including "inequality in economic structures and policies, in all forms of productive activities and in access to resources" and "inequality between men and women in the sharing of power and decision-making at all levels" (United Nations, 1995a). Under these concerns the following strategic objectives were stated:

+ eliminate occupational segregation and all forms of employment discrimination;
+ take measures to ensure women's equal access to and full participation in power structures and decision-making;
+ increase women's capacity to participate in decision-making and leadership.

As the leading public sector employer in many countries, the public service has a clear responsibility to work towards the attainment of these objectives.

Many countries of the Commonwealth have also ratified the Convention on the Elimination of all Forms of Discrimination against Women (CEDAW), which commits governments to passing laws to remove "women's subordinate status and promote setting up of institutions that further women's advancement" (CEDAW, 1995).

Development of Theoretical Approaches to Advancing Gender Equality

The United Nations Decade for the Advancement of Women (1975-1985) encouraged UN agencies, national governments, and NGOs to develop projects and programmes that would improve the economic and social position of women. The demand for policy attention to women's needs in development was often framed in terms of access or 'integration' to a range of development policy-making and project institutions. The implicit assumption behind many of these policies was that women's main problem in developing countries was insufficient participation in an otherwise benevolent process of growth and development.

The Women in Development (WID) approach was premised on this assumption and on the underlying rationale that women were an untapped resource that could provide an economic contribution to development. The thinking behind the WID approach was strongly affected by the assumption that heavy investment in education systems and in the development of highly trained workers and managers would result in the transformation of predominantly agricultural societies into ones which were industrialised and modernised. It was assumed that women and men would benefit equally from these changes.

This assumption began to be questioned in the 1980s, however, as the relative position of women over the two decades of modernisation had not only shown very little improvement, but had actually declined in some sectors. Gradually, it became widely recognised that women's experience of development was different from that of men, and research began to focus on women's views, opinions and experiences.

The gender and development (GAD) approach was offered as an alternative to the WID approach. This approach questioned the previous tendency to view women's problems in terms of their sex i.e. their biological distinctions from men – rather than in terms of their gender i.e. the social relationship between men and women in which women have been subordinated and oppressed. The GAD approach also emphasises the importance of taking into consideration class and race distinctions, and intra-class/race variations as these relate to gender.

The GAD approach supports the WID view that women must be given the opportunity to participate on equal terms in all aspects of life, but its primary focus is to examine the gendered power structures of society. The state is expected to assist in this process of promotion of women's emancipation, and has been called upon, for example, to assume the responsibility of facilitating women's participation in the productive sphere by providing social services such as child care, which women in many countries provide on a voluntary or private basis. The GAD approach also places strong emphasis on legal reform.

The shift in emphasis from WID to GAD has the potential for more efficient use of development resources, and greater long-term benefits, since a major objective of the GAD approach is ensuring that women are empowered to affect development planning and implementation. In the GAD approach, women are viewed as agents of change rather than as passive recipients of development assistance. However, government practice has sometimes been slow to follow this shift in theoretical perspective (Commonwealth Secretariat, 1999b).

Gender mainstreaming involves, among other things:
+ focusing attention on the vital roles played by women as well as men in sustainable development, and ensuring that these roles are acknowledged;
+ ensuring that women's and men's voices are heard equally and that both women and men participate in making decisions that affect their lives, at all levels: the national level of government and the public service, the local and community level, and the family and personal level;
+ ensuring that, in all sectors, policy is developed based on sex-disaggregated data and an awareness that policy decisions impact on the lives of women and men in different ways;
+ ensuring that the delivery of government services is equitable and that resources are allocated to women and men – and among different social groupings according to age, race/ethnicity, class/caste and other differences – on an equitable basis;
+ empowering women to define and articulate their needs and aspirations, and to acquire skills, experience and self confidence in order to participate equally at all levels; and
+ ensuring that language used in policy statements and other documents is gender sensitive and inclusive, and does not imply bias towards a male perception of society.

3 Institutional Framework for Mainstreaming Gender in Public Service Personnel Management

The Gender Management System

The Commonwealth has developed the Gender Management System (GMS) as a means of mainstreaming gender throughout national governments. The GMS is defined as:

"a network of structures, mechanisms and processes put in place within an existing organisational framework [such as a national government], to guide, plan, monitor and evaluate the process of mainstreaming gender into all areas of the organisation's work, in order to achieve greater gender equity within the context of sustainable development…"

Commonwealth Secretariat, 1999a

Enabling Environment

A programme of gender mainstreaming in the public service requires a positive enabling environment including political will at the highest level, legal and administrative frameworks that are conducive to gender equality, and sufficient resources for the programme's implementation. Where any of these elements is lacking, lobbying, advocacy and awareness raising are necessary on the part of the National Women's Machinery or Women's Bureau, as well as other interested parties, to bring about the requisite change in consciousness for a suitably enabling environment.

Public service commissions and central personnel agencies can, through their supervisory role of the whole administration system, play an important role in bringing about this change in consciousness by identifying targets, giving policy advice to stakeholders regarding gender mainstreaming, and securing the implementation of gender-positive policies.

The Structures of a GMS

The interrelated structures of the GMS are designed to provide a strong and sustainable institutional framework for gender mainstreaming.

A central component of the GMS is the Gender Management Team, which consists of the Permanent Secretary of core government ministries, such as Women's or Gender Affairs, Finance, Development Planning, Justice, and the Public Service. The Gender Management Team would also include at least one representative of civil society, such as the head of the National Commission on Gender Equality.

The role of the Gender Management Team is to provide leadership for the mainstreaming of gender in the core ministries, and establish broad operational policies, indicators to measure the effectiveness of those policies, and timeframes for their implementation.

A GMS also includes other institutional arrangements for mainstreaming gender:

✦ Gender Focal Points – two or more designated senior staff members in each core and line ministry, whose role is to serve as in-house gender experts, share information on gender issues, and promote gender mainstreaming in their ministries;

✦ an Inter-Ministerial Steering Committee whose representatives are the Gender Focal Points in each ministry;

✦ a Commission or Council on Gender Equality; and

✦ a Parliamentary Gender Caucus consisting of gender-aware parliamentarians.

Public service commissions and central personnel agencies have a key role to play in setting up the various institutional structures of the Gender Management System. While the Gender Focal Points will be nominated by their respective departments, public service commissions and/or central personnel agencies can work with the Lead Agency, i.e., the National Women's Machinery (Women's Bureau or Ministry of Women's Affairs) to develop these institutional structures and ensure that nominations are forthcoming for the various positions.

The GMS structures function within the context of the particular organisation or agency in which they are established. In the case of public service management systems, this context is undergoing change and varies according to particular national circumstances.

Public service commissions and central personnel agencies are also among the ministries affected by the national Gender Action Plan and by mainstreaming gender within their own ongoing activities.

Structure and functions of public service management systems

In many Commonwealth countries, public service commissions have been fashioned mainly after the British Civil Service Commission. For all but a few Commonwealth countries, provisions relating to public service commissions were written into the founding constitutions on achieving independence. In East and Southern African Commonwealth countries, for example, public service commissions all have their functions succinctly spelt out in the constitution.

An important function of the public service commission is to uphold and protect the public service's traditional values, namely, neutrality, selection by merit, and probity and integrity. Each of these values has a particular gender dimension.

Neutrality: One of the aims in creating public service commissions in Commonwealth countries at the time of independence was to safeguard the political neutrality of the public service. For this reason, public services can be resistant to changes made by governments to their status and functioning (Polidano and Manning, 1996: 7-9). So even when there is political will towards adopting more gender-aware practices and approaches, change may not come rapidly.

Selection by merit: The merit principle is regarded as one of the foundation stones of the public service. However, it raises some important issues when looked at from a gender perspective. In many countries of the Commonwealth, educational and career opportunities have over several generations been far more available to men than to women. Although women are catching up with men in education and work experience in a number of countries, a narrow application of the merit principle, based only on the past training and experience of the applicant, could nevertheless result in a disproportionate number of jobs being awarded to male applicants.

Two approaches may be adopted to correct this imbalance without prejudicing the merit principle: positive action and affirmative action. Positive action means taking special steps to encourage people from under-represented groups (e.g., women) to apply for a post, and to ensure that the recruitment and selection process is welcoming to them. However, at the point of selection, all candidates are treated equally. This means that there is no preference given to any group. Affirmative action means that the interview board selects a candidate from an under-represented group (e.g., a woman) where he or she is suitably qualified for the position (based on criteria set by the board), in preference to any other candidate who also meets the requirements.

Only if the selected candidate is less well-qualified than another can it be argued that the merit principle is being breached. However, merit is a function not only of the past experience of the applicant, but also of the stated requirements of any specified job. The inclusion in the job specifications of a requirement that the incumbent be aware of and experienced in dealing with gender issues would serve to increase the numbers of decision-makers who are gender-sensitive and can take gender-informed decisions.

Probity and integrity: These traditional values of the public service can be brought to bear on gender mainstreaming through the understanding that women's rights are human rights, and that the denial of equality for women is a breach of their human rights. Probity and integrity require a respect for human rights.

Most public service commissions work in collaboration with a government ministry, variously referred to as the ministry of the public service or central personnel office. The central personnel office is part of the executive and fully accountable to the government. It deals with matters not under the remit of the public service commission, which can include job creation and classification, staff training and development, and determining pay and conditions of work (Polidano and Manning, 1996: 11).

Increasingly, a third set of players in public service personnel management is made up of line ministries and departments, to whom some decisions relating to staff appointments, promotions, training and discipline are delegated.

There are therefore three strategic points of entry for gender mainstreaming in the management of public service personnel: the Public Service Commission itself, the central personnel office, and the line departments.

Between them, these three players are responsible for three major areas of personnel management, namely appointments, promotions and setting terms and conditions of employment; discipline; and staff training.

Public service reform

Many Commonwealth governments are engaged in a vigorous process of reform in their public services. The Commonwealth Initiative for Public Service Reform involves, among other things, a shifting of emphasis from a regulative to a performance-oriented approach, with the use of improved performance management systems to ensure that career advancement is linked to high performance. Another aspect of this reform is that power to make decisions is increasingly being delegated from the public service commission to other agencies. Depending on how advanced the process of public service reform is in a given country, the three players will share their responsibilities in different ways.

The task of mainstreaming gender in the public service cannot be accomplished through the public service commission alone; the involvement is also required of the central personnel office and each of the line ministries where personnel decisions are taken. Of particular importance are such core ministries as Finance, Legal/Justice, and Development Planning.

A performance management approach to public service management, such as that being adopted by many Commonwealth governments, is premised on the following key elements:
+ timely and accurate flows of *information* about what is being achieved in the work of the public service;
+ setting clear *standards* of performance and establishing the boundaries of acceptable behaviour;
+ clearly defining areas of *responsibility*, such that staff are aware of what is expected of them;
+ systems of *accountability*, such that good work is recognised and rewarded, and unacceptable performance sanctioned.

The adoption of a performance management approach provides a point of entry for gender mainstreaming through the integration of a gender awareness into each of these four elements. The GMS mechanisms provide a means of achieving this.

GMS Mechanisms

Gender analysis

Gender analysis is the process by which the differential impact on women and men of development policies can be discerned. It involves the collection and use of sex-disaggregated data which reveals the different status, conditions, roles and responsibilities of women and men. This data is fed into the policy process, to enable assessments of the impact of existing policies and programmes on gender inequalities. Gender analysis also involves assessing how gender-inequitable power relations may impact on the achievement of a range of development goals including the goal of gender equality.

Gender analysis needs to be both quantitative and qualitative. The use of gender-sensitive indicators in such areas as demographics, patterns of human settlement, households and families, education, health, economic activity, access to land and credit, legal rights, gender-based violence, and macroeconomics can provide useful quantitative data which should be complemented by qualitative data including historical and socio-cultural analyses that help to clarify the 'why' as well as the 'what' of gender differences in a given society.

Management Information System

The Management Information System is the repository and clearing house for all information relating to the establishment and functioning of the GMS. Its function is to gather, synthesise and disseminate information on the goals, activities and achievements of the GMS and on other topics relating to gender mainstreaming and the advancement of gender equality and equity.

The Management Information System works closely with the government statistical agency or census bureau. It promotes and develops the use of sex-disaggregated data based on gender-sensitive indicators to provide material for gender impact analysis, policy appraisal, and monitoring and evaluation. It also works closely with the government information agency and with media contacts to disseminate information regarding gender mainstreaming and the GMS. This may be achieved through a monthly or quarterly information sheet, bulletin or newsletter. Innovative methods for collecting, documenting, storing, retrieving and disseminating information should be devised. Appropriate resources should be made available for such efforts, which play a key role in transforming the institutional belief systems and organisational culture (Commonwealth Secretariat, 1999a).

The public service ministry or commission should work closely with the Management Information System, which would normally be set up by the GMS lead agency, namely the Ministry of Gender Affairs or Women's Bureau. The public service ministry should provide sex-disaggregated information on staffing at all levels, and on the gender implications of staffing and personnel policies. In return, the Management Information System should provide the public service ministry with information on the establishment and functioning of the GMS in core and line ministries.

Performance Appraisal System

A gender-aware performance appraisal system which rewards the advancement of gender equality and equity is one of the critical levers through which organisational change can be brought about.

The central personnel office, public service commission or ministry of public service can play a key role in ensuring that the performance appraisal systems in use in the public service are gender-sensitive. The system(s) should be able to measure changes in individual and departmental standards of achievement of the goals of the Gender Management System, including the extent to which individual staff members have acquired gender awareness (e.g. through training) and have applied such awareness in their work (e.g. through the achievement of gender goals or the institution of gender-specific programmes). This information should form one of the criteria for career advancement.

Incentives do not necessarily have to be financial; for example, a gender awareness award of merit, publicised through the

Management Information System, could help to transform the institutional culture to one that is more gender-aware and more supportive of gender equity goals (Commonwealth Secretariat, 1999a).

Gender training

Gender training is necessary in order to build capacity in gender analysis and gender planning, to raise levels of gender awareness and to increase gender sensitivity. Among the various types of training offered to public service employees by the public service commission or central personnel office, gender awareness training should be included as a matter of course.

It is of prime importance that the members of the Gender Management Team and the Gender Focal Points be aware of and sensitive to gender issues. It will therefore be necessary, as a high priority, to provide gender awareness training to these staff members so they can effectively fill their leadership role in gender mainstreaming.

A number of measures should be taken to improve the quality and scope of gender training:

✦ capacity-building in gender awareness, analysis and planning should be undertaken throughout government structures, not only in the social sectors;
✦ gender training should include both more general gender sensitisation exercises and substantive, sector-specific training exercises directly related to knowledge gaps identified by policy-makers themselves;
✦ gender training should be regular and ongoing;
✦ gender training should include briefing on the GMS, explaining its mainstreaming aim and its component parts;
✦ since the promotion of gender awareness is a cumulative process, gender training should not be seen as a 'one-off' exercise but should be provided at regular intervals in an ongoing programme (Commonwealth Secretariat, 1999a).

4

Processes for Mainstreaming Gender in Public Service Personnel Management

Gender Analysis

The first stage in the process of mainstreaming in public service personnel management involves a gender-based analysis of the existing situation. Timely and reliable statistics are the foundation of sound gender analysis. Without adequate, reliable and valid statistical descriptions, inequities can be perpetuated. For example, the role of women in decision-making positions in an organisation's functioning is generally less well recognised than the role of men. Without accurate sex-disaggregated data, the individual contributions of women in the public sector tend to remain invisible.

Qualitative gender analysis involves asking questions about women's and men's life experiences in all aspects of political, public and private life, and about how and why the current situation has arisen. Such analysis is complementary to, and to some extent dependent upon, quantitative analysis involving the use of statistical information.

Gender-sensitive indicators

A *gender-sensitive indicator* is defined as a piece of statistical information on some aspect of women's lives, status or situation vis-à-vis that of men, and on how that situation is changing over time. Such indicators are necessary tools for measuring progress towards attaining the objective of gender equality and ensuring that the benefits of development are shared equitably. It is important to ensure that government collectors of statistics, both in a central statistical agency and in specific sectors, develop and gather indicators on a gender-aware basis.

Indicators can be used, for example, to determine how women and men are recruited in the public service – at which level and in what numbers relative to each other. Research should be carried out to account for any discrepancies in accession rates. The indicators should also show women and men's promotion rates in the different grades, and the reasons for discrepancies. Data on women should also be disaggregated according to marital status, so as to determine whether there are fewer married women in certain grades and, if so, why. Qualitative research would help to delineate whether the heavy workload of home, office, and extra-curricular activities militates against women's promotional or accession rates.

Women should be seen not as a homogenous group but as reflecting the diversity of the entire national population. Therefore, data should also be disaggregated by age, race/ethnicity, class and disability in order to reveal the differential impact on women's lives not only of their gender but also of these other characteristics.

The first step is to obtain comprehensive sex-disaggregated data on the personnel of the public service at all levels including senior management, middle management, and professional, technical and support staff. This will reveal whether and where there are gender inequities and will assist the identification of strategies to correct the imbalances. The tendency is often for senior management to be dominated by men, and the lower echelons by women. However, this is changing in some countries and it is necessary to be aware of country-specific circumstances in determining appropriate strategies to advance gender equity and equality.

Based on the above analysis, the next step is to identify who the decision-makers are in public service management, ensure that women are well represented among their number, and that all, women and men, are experienced and/or trained in gender issues. Targets should be set to achieve this within a specified time frame.

It is also important to undertake a sex-disaggregated survey of the status of women and men in the broader society over an extended period of time, according to basic indicators of health, education, income, and political and economic participation. From this it is possible to identify the major areas of gender inequality, the historical reasons for these, and the strengths, weaknesses, opportunities and threats regarding the advancement of gender equality and equity. Data should again be disaggregated by age, race/ethnicity, class and disability.

Policy analysis

Existing personnel policies should be examined from a gender perspective to determine whether they are conducive to gender equality and equity. A useful approach to analysing government policies is to determine whether they are gender-neutral, gender-specific or gender-aware/redistributive/transformative, as follows:

✦ Gender-neutral policies are those that are seen as having no significant gender dimension. However, government policies seldom if ever have the same effect on women as they do on men, even if at first sight they may appear to exist in a context where gender is irrelevant. Thus policies which may appear to be gender-neutral are often in fact gender-blind, and are biased in favour of males because they presuppose that those involved in and affected by the policy are males, with male needs and interests.

✦ Gender-specific policies take into account gender differentials, and target women or men specifically, but leave the current distribution of resources and responsibilities intact.

✦ Gender-aware/redistributive/transformative policies seek to transform existing gender relations by changing the distribution of resources and responsibilities to make it more equitable. These policies are the most politically challenging, because they involve altering the existing balance of power between men and women, but they also go the furthest towards addressing not only practical gender needs but strategic gender interests as well (adapted from Kabeer, 1994).

In addition, a process of gender analysis should be initiated or supported on the part of each of the core and line ministries in terms of their broader sectoral policies, and how these impact on men and women in different ways.

Once these gender analyses have been carried out, new personnel policies need to be developed to address existing gender imbalances. And the policy development processes of core and line ministries need to be carried out with an awareness of the gender implications of specific sectoral policy options.

Sectoral analyses

The mainstreaming of gender in government involves putting into place a visible mechanism to co-ordinate and monitor the implementation of gender-related sectoral platforms of action which target critical areas of concern. Sectoral plans can then be consolidated into national action plans.

Major policy directions, prioritised goals, developed strategies and action plans for each sector must be included in gender-related development plans. This will ensure implementation of a gender-based approach. The public service can take a role in encouraging other related ministries to incorporate gender dimensions in their structures, policies and programmes. It is particularly important that this is done in the core ministries of finance, development planning and justice.

Legal framework: The legal framework that affects personnel management in the public service may include constitutional provisions (such as those concerning the public service commission) as well as particular pieces of legislation such as a Public Service Act or similar legal document. Often, this legal framework provides a general context and set of guiding principles under which particular policies regarding personnel management are developed by the government of the day.

The legal framework should be examined to determine to what extent it is or is not conducive to gender equality. Normally, a gender-positive law or principle is one which makes specific reference to gender equality or to prohibiting discrimination. Laws and principles that are silent on gender issues are not necessarily gender-neutral, but may serve to perpetuate gender inequities.

Where the legal framework is found to be wanting, efforts should be made towards constitutional reform or to a change in existing legislation. In many Commonwealth countries where public service reform programmes are under way, the Public Service Act or similar piece of legislation is being completely rewritten in order to effect the necessary reforms. This offers a good opportunity for mainstreaming gender issues into the new legislation. Public service commissions, central personnel departments and women's bureaux can take a lobbying and advocacy role to ensure that this happens.

Another important dimension of the legal framework is the administration of justice, in terms of both civil and criminal law. Issues with a critical gender dimension in these areas include:

+ violence against women, including domestic violence, physical and sexual abuse, coerced prostitution and trafficking in women, the sexual exploitation of the girl-child and sexual assault;
+ laws regarding sexual harassment;
+ the treatment of rape victims by police and other authorities;
+ women's access to land and resources; and
+ the rights of married women as compared to those of their husbands.

The ratification and implementation of international human rights agreements such as CEDAW is an important element of a national legal framework that is conducive to gender equality.

Macroeconomic policies: These are often seen as gender-neutral, but in fact impact on women and men in sometimes radically different ways. Gender mainstreaming means ensuring the participation of women as well as men in macroeconomic planning. Government should analyse, from a gender perspective, the overall impact of the economic structural adjustment programmes, especially in the public service where the reduction of numbers is proposed, and in the restructuring of public expenditures where gender equality and equity can be compromised.

Gender budgeting and gender accounting are processes that identify and monitor the flow of financial resources to determine their differential impacts, with a view to ensuring equal benefits and access for both men and women. Initiatives of this kind have provided useful information on the gender implications of macroeconomic policies in Australia, South Africa, and elsewhere

Initiatives are under way in a number of Commonwealth countries to integrate gender into the national budgetary process, reflecting the need to incorporate gender awareness into economic development efforts.

Development planning: Mainstream development theories, policies and strategies have tended to analyse poverty through a gender-blind or a gender-neutral lens. However, most approaches are in fact not neutral because they assume the male actor as standard and representative of the human race. Consequently, gender-neutral policies address women's lived experiences, needs, interests and constraints only to the extent to which they conform to or overlap with the norms set by the male actor. Within the context of poverty analysis, this leads to misdiagnoses of poverty through the omission of its gendered dimensions.

Public service planners have come to realise that development goals will only be reached by securing the active economic involvement of women as well as men in a balanced way. Because women are mostly the poor, plans and goals should be women-oriented. This means women must be brought into the mainstream of economic development so that both women and men are in a position to play a productive role. Women's right to economic empowerment should be explicitly recognised in poverty alleviation programmes which should be integrated into overall economic planning.

Education: Advancing gender equality in the education sector is of strategic importance to the public service, since the education sector is preparing the political leaders and civil servants of tomorrow. A gender approach is particularly appropriate in this sector because, in some regions of the Commonwealth, girls are outperforming boys at secondary school, and more women than men are entering the lower ranks of the public service, while elsewhere it is women who are at a disadvantage. Gender analysis makes these differences visible.

Gender-sensitive indicators of enrolment rates in tertiary education (from where the public service accesses its recruitment input) need to be subjected to analysis to determine drop-out rates and the reasons for them, and appropriate policies designed in response. Pass rates by sex in various subjects and at various levels of education, and the socialisation and streaming of girls and boys into particular, often stereotyped subjects are areas of particular relevance.

Gender equity targets are frequently set only for managerial positions, ignoring the professional and technical fields. In some countries there are very few women in these fields at the entry level. The problem emanates partly from differential socialisation processes and partly from covert and overt biases in the education system. A closer look at the mechanism of recruitment into these fields should be undertaken. Collaboration is required between the public service and the education sector to examine the indicators of gender disparities and jointly devise strategies to promote greater gender equality and equity.

Policy Development

The process of policy development is changing. Governments have recognised the need for gender-aware policy development and are taking steps to ensure it. It is now harder for public officials to make policies based on data which is not gender-disaggregated without prior consultation with stakeholders, and to hand down solutions without prior discussion. Women have become more organised through activism and networking from the grassroots to the pinnacle of public services at the national level, and are demanding a greater degree of consultation on policy issues.

Setting gender targets

Commonwealth Heads of Government have endorsed a target of no less than 30 per cent women in decision-making in the political, public and private spheres by the year 2005[1]. The Beijing Platform for Action targets a 50 per cent figure of women holding managerial and decision-making positions by the year 2000. Individual governments committed to gender mainstreaming will also set their own targets, consistent with national circumstances and priorities. Public service commissions and central personnel offices will play a vital role both in setting national targets and in co-ordinating, overseeing and monitoring their implementation.

Personnel management policies should reflect these targets and set up specific mechanisms for their realisation. A broad-based approach is needed that takes into account the multiple dimensions and complexities of the issues being dealt with. Targets should be as specific as possible, e.g., not just '35 per cent of staff should be women', but '35 per cent of senior managers at grades x – y, in z ministry, should be women by the year 2000'.

In setting targets for gender equity it is important to take into account current circumstances, and aim for a realistic, achievable target. More will be accomplished by realising a relatively modest goal than by setting a wide range of far-reaching targets and failing to meet any of them.

Gender-Related Policy Issues in Personnel Management

In mainstreaming gender into public service personnel management there are a number of policy issues that impinge upon the activities of the three main players:

Staffing and conditions of employment

Eliminating gender-based discrimination as regards pay: A policy of equal work for equal pay should be applied to eliminate gender-based differentials in pay within a specific job. A further step is the adoption of an approach whereby different jobs of comparable worth are rewarded with equal pay, since they are of equal value to the employer. This will help to correct pay differentials between different jobs that are seen as gender-specific (i.e., for men only or for women only) – a major source of the gender 'wage gap'. Encouraging women to enter fields traditionally reserved for men, and vice versa, will further help to redress this imbalance (IDLL, 1996: 3.3.1).

Ensuring an adequate gender balance in decision-making roles: the Commonwealth has set the target of at least 30 per cent women in decision-making positions in government by the year 2005. Governments that are already near that target are urged to aim for a 50-50 gender balance in decision-making.

In order to achieve this, governments should take active measures to encourage women to apply for senior and decision-making posts (positive action) and, where possible and consistent with the merit principle, hire women into these posts (affirmative action). Job specifications should be gender-sensitive and not assume, for example, that the incumbent will be male (IDLL, 1996: 3.3.4).

In many countries, recruitment policies tend to exclude women from certain jobs and this exclusion is exacerbated by male bias manifested in the composition of selection panels. A male-dominated interview panel may apply excessive scrutiny and pressure to women and expect them to perform better than their male counterparts. Therefore it is important to ensure that the decision-makers on matters of hiring and promotion (including interview boards) include a fair and representative number of women and gender-aware people.

Criticism has been levelled at the use of seniority as a criterion for promotion in the public service, as opposed to the application of the merit principle. Historically, women have not had education and experience at the same level as men in most countries, so the use of seniority as a criterion for promotion exercises discriminates against them. With the current programmes of public service reform, the tendency is to abandon seniority in favour of the merit principle; nevertheless, care needs to be taken through the various stages of promotion – suitability boards, interviewing and short listing panels – to obviate the use of seniority to the detriment of merit.

The broadening of career paths, so that women may move from one path to another without loss of seniority or other penalties, will help to facilitate the movement of women into job areas traditionally reserved for men, and vice versa (IDLL, 1996: 3.3.2).

Determining equitable conditions of employment: The terms and conditions relating to public service employment may include provisions that discriminate against women or that fail to recognise differentials in the life courses and experiences of women and men. Allowance must be made for the fact that women in the workplace often carry a double load: their employment and their family responsibilities, which can include housework, pregnancy, child-bearing and child care (IDLL, 1996: 2.1). Terms and conditions which ignore such differentials may well be discriminatory. Pension benefits are another area in which there may be discrimination: the question of whether women and men receive the same levels of benefits from the pensions policy should be addressed.

Efforts should be made by the central personnel agency to provide on-site child-care facilities for the children of working mothers. Working hours should be sufficiently flexible to allow mothers to schedule their working day in harmony with school or other arrangements for their children, and to allow fathers to carry out these tasks as well (IDLL, 1996: 2.3).

Discipline

Ensuring disciplinary measures are devised and applied equitably: Care should be taken that codes of conduct do not contain 'hidden' discrimination, for example by applying a double standard in codes of behaviour or by imposing more severe penalties for misconduct in job areas normally occupied by women.

Eliminating sexual harassment: Many women face gender-based harassment at their workplace. This contributes to creating a working environment that is not welcoming to women. Codes of conduct for the public service should include the prohibition of and penalties for sexual and other forms of gender-based harassment.

Training and capacity building

Training in the public service has two distinct gender dimensions. The first has to do with building the capacity for gender analysis, planning and policy development, and gender-aware management and decision-making. The second has to do with access to career-related training in diverse fields; women and men do not always have equal access to training opportunities, and may suffer impediments to career choice and advancement as a result.

Gender awareness training: In mainstreaming gender in the public service, it is necessary as a first priority to ensure that the key decision-makers at senior levels are gender-sensitive. Gender awareness training should therefore be provided for the Permanent Secretaries of all core and line ministries (except of course those who have already received such training or who are conversant and experienced in dealing with gender issues). It is particularly important that the heads of such core ministries as Finance, Planning, Personnel and Justice are gender-sensitive.

Gender awareness skills should be a requirement for all those in management positions. Gender training is a means of building a critical mass of women (and men) imbued with gender-related skills and knowledge, both for use in their own professional responsibilities and to impart to others who are thus likewise empowered to become agents for change.

The ultimate goal is to raise the level of gender awareness of as many staff as possible, particularly those in key decision-making roles. However, in devising and running gender awareness training programmes, the principle of 'less is more' should be borne in mind: rather than attempting to achieve full gender awareness and equity throughout the public service overnight, training should incorporate an understanding of the prevailing socio-cultural environment and should be tailored to specific, realistic goals and targets.

The training of trainers is another important strategy to maximise the propagation of gender awareness throughout the public service. In some countries, there is potential for the training division within the public service to organise courses in gender sensitivity and gender analysis in collaboration with centres for gender and development at institutes of higher education.

Ensuring equity in the availability of training options: It is important to ensure that women and men receive equal opportunities for training – including on-the-job training – to ensure that they are equally competitive in their respective fields. Training is a particularly useful indicator of progress towards gender equality and equity since it is readily accountable, in terms of expenditures, time, number of women and men being trained, and level of skills or knowledge being imparted.

The training should itself be gender-sensitive. For example, women who are receiving management training may benefit from training in specific areas like leadership and assertiveness and in understanding the values that permeate male-dominated areas of society and of the public service. Part of the process of mainstreaming gender in the public service entails questioning the prevalent values and behaviours regarding gender.

Establishing partnerships with NGOs and the academic community: Women's non-governmental organisations can be a useful resource and partner in gender mainstreaming. Networking and active dialogue with such organisations and with the academic community will provide valuable input on such questions as providing gender awareness training, the development of gender-aware personnel management and sectoral policies, and making equal use of the existing capacities, skills and knowledge of women and men in the national context.

Incentives and sanctions

As public services move from a regulative to a performance-based approach, the scope is enlarged for applying incentives to encourage gender mainstreaming and/or sanctions on managers who practice gender discrimination.

Incentives for good performance: Once targets have been set for advancing gender equality, managers who achieve those targets can be rewarded through an established and credible performance appraisal system. These rewards do not necessarily have to be financial; in fact, research suggests that recognition and feedback may be more effective than money as motivators (Jorm, Hunt and Manning, 1996: 40).

Non-financial rewards can include certificates, awards of merit and medals or pins. For such awards to maintain credibility, they shoul indicate that recognition of good performance has come from the highest levels, namely the President's or Prime Minister's Office, or the minister of the relevant department (Jorm, Hunt and Manning, 1996: 42).

Sanctions for practising discrimination: If managers practise gender-based discrimination or fail to implement an equal employment opportunities policy, a first step would be to determine the cause of the discrimination or failure. Is the manager gender-aware? If not, could the situation be improved through gender-awareness training? Ultimately, such discrimination or failure could result in other sanctions, such as transference to another post, reduction in grade level, or disciplinary action (Jorm, Hunt and Manning, 1996: 47).

Equal employment opportunities policy

The best way to ensure that the above issues are addressed is through the adoption and implementation of a comprehensive Equal Employment Opportunities policy.

Policy Appraisal

Policy appraisal is the term given to the analysis of proposed or existing policy before implementation. Gender-based policy appraisal entails assessing the differential impact of policies and programmes on women and men. Some of the questions that can be asked in the process of a gender-based policy appraisal are as follows:

+ How many and which women and men have been consulted about this policy and at what levels?
+ How many and which women and men are included in its implementation?
+ How many and which women and men will benefit from this policy, and by how much?
+ Does this policy have deleterious effects on women or men?
+ How should this policy be changed to correct any imbalances?
+ How does this policy advance the government's overall objectives and international commitments regarding equality and equity between women and men?
+ What obstacles might prevent women's equitable participation in the policy and an equitable outcome for women? How can these obstacles be overcome?

Gender Action Plan

The outcome of a gender-based appraisal of personnel management policies should be a plan of action to mainstream gender within the public service. The plan could include the following:

+ action to realise established targets for numbers of women in decision-making positions in the public service;
+ action to eliminate gender-based discrimination in matters of appointments, promotions, pay, conditions of employment and disciplinary procedures;
+ action to provide gender awareness training where needed, especially for heads of department in the core ministries, line department heads, managers and decision-makers throughout the public service;
+ action to set up institutional structures for the promotion, implementation and monitoring of gender mainstreaming in all core and line ministries (for example, a Gender Management System) and to supervise and monitor the functioning of these structures;
+ action to ensure that gender issues are integrated in the development of core and sectoral work plans and budget allocations;
+ action to establish or strengthen working partnerships between the public service and women's non-governmental organisations;
+ action to establish or improve monitoring and reporting systems, to ensure that information on gender issues is timely and accurate; and
+ action to provide incentives to, and/or impose sanctions on, government departments to encourage a full implementation o plans for gender equality.

Monitoring and Evaluation

Once the plan has been implemented, it is of course necessary to determine how successful it has been and draw lessons from it for the next planning cycle. Monitoring and evaluation of the outcomes of policies offer opportunities for further improving policy through feedback using statistical and economic analyses. These analyses can take various forms: cost/benefit analysis, impac assessment, and mechanisms for quantitative and qualitative progress measurement.

The basic tools of these analyses are similar to those used in the gender analysis and project appraisal phases of the cycle; they include the use of gender-sensitive indicators complemented by qualitative research and analysis to account for differences and disparities in gender issues. Thus the monitoring and evaluation phase of one policy cycle feeds directly into the initial analysis phase of the next cycle.

Internal and External Communications

An efficient and reliable communications system is of vital importance in undertaking a process of gender mainstreaming. Communications channels serve two important functions:

+ They provide a means of monitoring and evaluating progress; accurate data on current circumstances is necessary for the development of effective policy options for the future.
+ They provide a means of communicating changes in policy, both internally within government and also externally to the broader civil society; this is essential, in the first instance, for the effective implementation of the policy, and secondly for reasons of transparency, public awareness and acceptance.

Notes

This was the target set at the 1996 Commonwealth Women's Affairs Ministers Meeting in Port of Spain, Trinidad and Tobago. The target was endorsed by Commonwealth Heads of Government at their 1997 summit in Edinburgh.

References

CEDAW (1995). "Contributions of the Committee to International Conferences." New York: UN, Report by the Committee on the Elimination of Discrimination against Women. CEDAW/C/1995.

Commonwealth Secretariat (1999a). *Gender Management System Handbook. Gender Management System Series.* London.

Commonwealth Secretariat (1999b). *Gender Mainstreaming in Education: A Reference Manual for Governments and Other Stakeholders, Gender Management System Series.* Authors: Leo-Rhynie, E and the Institute of Development and Labour Law, University of Cape Town. London.

Commonwealth Secretariat (1999c). *Gender Mainstreaming in the Public Service: A Reference Manual for Governments and Other Stakeholders, Gender Management System Series.* London.

Commonwealth Secretariat (1997). *The Commonwealth At the Summit, Volume 2: Communiqués of Commonwealth Heads of Government Meetings 1987-1995).* London.

Commonwealth Secretariat (1995a). *The 1995 Commonwealth Plan of Action on Gender and Development.* London.

Commonwealth Secretariat (1995b). *Working towards Gender Equality.* London.

Dodoo, R (1994). *The Civil Service Reform Programme.* Paper commissioned by Atlas Conference.

"Gender, Politics and Democracy". *Southern Africa Feminist Review* Vol. 1. No. 2.

Government of Canada (1996). *Gender-Based Analysis – A Guide for Policy-Makers.* Ottawa: Status of Women Canada.

Government of Zimbabwe (1984). *Equal Opportunities for Women, in the Civil Service.* Programme Action, Cabinet Office.

Government of Zimbabwe (1995). *First Report on the Convention on the Elimination of all forms of Discrimination against Women.* Harare

IDLL (1996). "Equal Employment Opportunities Policy as Regards Gender for Commonwealth Countries". Institute of Development and Labour Law, University of Cape Town. London: Commonwealth Secretariat consultancy paper.

Jorm, N; Hunt, J and Manning, N (1996). *Working Towards Results Managing Individual Performance in the Public Service.* London: Commonwealth Secretariat.

Kabeer, N (1994). "Gender-aware policy and planning: a social relations perspective", in MacDonald, M (ed.), *Gender Planning in Development Agencies*. Oxford: Oxfam.

Kaul, M (1995). *From Problem to Solution: Commonwealth Strategies for Reform*. London: Commonwealth Secretariat.

Made, P A and Matambanadzo, I (1996). *Beyond Beijing: Strategies and Visions Towards Women's Equality*. Harare: SADC Press Trust.

Moser, C (1989). "Gender Planning in the Third World: Meeting Practical and Strategic Gender needs," in *World Development* Vol. 17.

Nicholson, L (1994). *Interpreting Gender*. SIGNS.

Polidano, C and Manning, N (1996). *Redrawing the Lines: Service Commissions and the Delegation of Personnel Management*. London: Commonwealth Secretariat.

Russo, S *et al* (1989). *Gender Issues in Agriculture*. USAID.

SADC Secretariat (1997). *Into the Future: Gender and SADC*. Gaborone, Botswana.

Sen, G and Grown, C (1987). *Development Crises and Alternative Visions Third World Women's Perspective*. Monthly Review Press.

United Nations Development Programme (1990, 1995, 1997). *Human Development Report*. New York.

United Nations Development Programme (1991). *Focus on Women: United Nations Fund for Women*. New York.

UNICEF (1994). *A Review of the Social Dimensions of Adjustment in Zimbabwe 1990-94*. New York.

United Nations (1995a). *The Beijing Declaration and Platform for Action*. New York.

United Nations (1995b). *World Summit for Social Development: The Copenhagen Declaration*. New York.

United Nations (1994). *World Social Situation in the 1990s*.

Williams, G and Harvey, C (1998). "Gender Management Systems in Higher Education in the Commonwealth and Other Countries". Commonwealth Secretariat consultancy paper. London.

World Bank (1992). *Poverty Reduction Hand Book*. The World Bank, Washington, DC.

World Bank (1990). *World Development Report: Poverty*. Oxford University Press.

Appendix *Glossary of terms*

Gender

Gender can be defined as the set of characteristics, roles and behaviour patterns that distinguish women from men which are constructed not biologically but socially and culturally. The sex of an individual is biologically determined, whereas gender characteristics are socially constructed, a product of nurturing, conditioning, and socio-cultural norms and expectations. These characteristics change over time and from one culture to another. The concept of gender refers not only to women and men but, importantly to the relations of power between them. Gender relations are constantly being renegotiated in the context of changing political, economic, social, and cultural environments at the local, national and international level.

Gender analysis

Gender analysis is the qualitative and quantitative analysis of any information from a gender perspective, in order to draw out gender imbalances and inequities, and expose instances of gender discrimination. It involves collecting sex-disaggregated data to be fed into the policy process, and assessing the impact of existing policies and programmes on gender inequalities. It also involves assessing how gender-inequitable power relations may impact on the achievement of a range of development goals including the goal of gender equality.

Gender equality/equity

Gender equality can be understood in two ways: firstly, *formal equality* means treating everyone identically, regardless of circumstances. It is premised on the theory that all people are equal, and that treating all people in the same way is therefore fair. *Substantive equality*, on the other hand, is concerned with arriving at equality of outcomes rather than with giving identical treatment. This is the essence of gender equity (Status of Women Canada, 1996). Women's gender roles often prevent them from accessing resources and opportunities, even when these are offered without overt discrimination to either sex. In recognising the differential impact on women and men of policies which may appear to be non-discriminatory, gender equity involves taking whatever steps are necessary to ensure that women and men benefit equally from resources and opportunities.

Gender mainstreaming

Gender mainstreaming means ensuring that a gender perspective is included in the formulation and implementation of all government policies, programmes and decisions. It also includes extending a gender awareness to the broader civil society.

Gender-sensitive indicator

A gender-sensitive indicator is defined as a piece of statistical information on some aspect of women's lives, status or situation vis-à-vis that of men, and on how that situation is changing over time. Such indicators are necessary tools for measuring progress towards attaining the objective of gender equality and ensuring that the benefits of development are shared equitably.